AF270412

DICK TERMES

DICK TERMES

Black Hills Artist and Visionary

BY CRAIG VOLK

WITH AN INTRODUCTION BY **BILL FLEMING**

PHOTOGRAPHY BY **BONNY FLEMING**

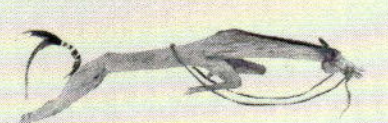

SOUTH DAKOTA HISTORICAL SOCIETY PRESS   PIERRE

© 2024 by the South Dakota Historical Society Press

All rights reserved. This book or portions thereof in any form whatsoever may not be reproduced without the expressed written approval of the South Dakota Historical Society Press, Pierre, S.Dak. 57501.

This publication is funded, in part, by Verna Kay Bormann, the City of Deadwood, and the Deadwood Historic Preservation Commission.

CIP information is available upon request

Printed in Canada

The paper in this book meets the guidelines for permanence and durability of the Committee on Production Guidelines for Book Longevity of the Council on Library Resources.

Design by Richard Hendel

Please visit our website at sdhspress.com

28 27 26 25 24   1 2 3 4 5 6

To the

SOUTH DAKOTA ARTS COUNCIL

and its invaluable support to artists

young (and old) for over 50 years

CONTENTS

INTRODUCTION

The Black Hills Genius Who Stayed Home

BILL FLEMING

Clyfford Still and Jackson Pollock are acknowledged geniuses in American Art History, each playing a key role in the innovation and development of a completely unforeseen genre of Visual Art: Abstract Expressionism. Most of us attuned to world culture are familiar with these two and their work. But somewhat fewer of us realize and appreciate that Still and Pollock came from North Dakota and Wyoming respectively, and that the average citizen of those two states probably does not really care for the paintings of their celebrated native sons. That was why they went to New York, at least for a while, to rub elbows with people who understood and could influence and promote what they were doing with their radical innovations.

It is a familiar story: talent from the boondocks bound for the big city to make it happen. But Richard ("Dick") Termes (pronounced Term-iss) is a different story. The very first edition of *Black Hills Monthly Magazine* featured Termes on its cover, with the headline "Dick Termes, the Black Hills Genius who stayed home." And why did he do that? Because he could. He was inventing something completely new—grounded in art history, to be sure, but so innovative that to this day it continues to defy easy categorization. But unlike Still and Pollock, Termes has taken great care to make sure that his fellow South Dakotans understand what he is up to. In fact, one might say that when it comes to Termes's art, the rest of the world is still trying to catch up with South Dakota.

So how does that work?

Here is the thing about Dick Termes in the canon of art history: it is not that he doesn't fit anywhere, but that he fits everywhere. Well, almost everywhere. Dick himself will tell you that while he understands and appreciates most of the historical western art history movements, he tends to shy away from Abstract Expressionism (and Expressionism in general) in his own explorations. Not always, but in general. That's because so much of Termes's work is about mind as opposed to heart. He will tell you that he prefers rationalism over emotionalism and sentimentality, that he's more about structure than gesture, and that in the context of plasticity, his picture space is decidedly more illusion and vision than surface plane affirmation and texture. But let's back up a bit and try to guess how Termes came to approach his paintings the way he does.

In very simple terms, much of the complexity of Western Civilization's history of painters and painting can be boiled down to a consideration of what artists call "picture space." In general, the manipulation of that space has to do with how the artist acknowledges (or sometimes ignores) the boundaries and surface of the paper, canvas, panel, wall, or whatever object they are painting on.

Rule of thumb: the more the painting's execution seems to feature the surface it is painted on, the more "modern" it probably is. In a nutshell that is what modern painting is all about: paint on the surface, as opposed to an illusion that makes viewers feel as though they are looking through a window, off into a distant land that is somehow "behind" the picture's surface and frame.

David Hockney reveals in his excellent book *Secret Knowledge: Rediscovering the Lost Techniques of the Old Masters* that Western Civilization's painters, from the Early Renaissance up to the introduction of photography, were working to accomplish the visual articulation of the photorealistic illusion (especially after the development of optical devices). It became the *de facto* standard against which almost all paintings and painters were measured. How real and convincing can you make your picture look? But once the camera that could nail it every time was invented, it was pretty much game over for most painters.

With optics, cameras, and photorealism came the various tools and techniques of linear perspective, allowing artists to arrange the objects on the surfaces of their pictures the way the camera does, so precisely that aside from the frame that bounds it, the physical object of the picture itself seems to disappear and only the illusion remains.

But that frame, what to do with it? Enter Dick Termes.

By the time Termes started his art studies, the Modern Art movement was not only well underway, but was in fact starting to run out of steam on most fronts. In Europe, Impressionism had morphed into Post-Impressionism, and then the Fauves, Proto-Cubists and Cubists, Surrealists, Expressionists, Neoplastisticists, and then of course, Dada.

But let's not go there, because we don't have to. It all came here, mostly to New York City and to some degree to San Francisco and Los Angeles, where Abstract Expressionism and the Americans had become the new driving force in Western Art, but at the same time seemed to many to be running the art car into an overly formulaic ditch.

Termes, like most of his generation, quickly realized that while there were now dozens, if not hundreds, of ways for him to approach his surface and subject matter, there was still one fundamental limitation that only the medium of motion picture film was just beginning to come to grips with: the edges of the surface itself. Even the gigantic screens in the movie theaters have them.

The trick in theaters is not unlike the gigantic canvases of the Abstract Expressionists or the Mexican muralists. To faithfully depict reality and fully engage the audience, those edges must go. The answer, it seemed, was to scale it all up, make it so big that the audience could become fully immersed in it without distraction from the outside world.

Stand up close to a Mark Rothko painting and the world of emotion contained in the piece is all you experience. Same with being in a big theater, with moving pictures on screen, a darkened room, and surround sound. The viewer becomes fully immersed in a separate reality for a while. Like magic. Total engagement.

In this context Termes's discovery is as simple as it is elegant. The surface does not have to be oversized, or dark, or comprised of constantly changing angles, perspectives, and points of view (as with Cubism). It just has to be—wait for it—*round*. Spherical, to be exact.

Once Termes hit on that ideal, all the prior modalities of painting—from cave walls to Picasso, Rembrandt, Turner, Mondrian, Monet, Magritte, and Matisse—became ripe for serious reexamination in his entirely new spherical picture space. Termespheres, where a picture is no longer just a little window into the world of an artist's imagination, but an entire new world unto itself.

And just as the whole universe (or perhaps even the multiverse) erupted from a singular super-high-energy point billions of years ago, so do the worlds of Termes spring forth from the mind of a high-energy genius in a charming little valley just south of Spearfish, South Dakota. Dick Termes, the Black Hills genius who stayed home.

 Richard Termes

PROLOGUE

Everyone who knows him knows this about him: he's a soft-spoken, affable man. He laughs easy and often. His fingers bow slightly inward from a lifetime of caressing his curved canvases. While pursuing his MFA, a professor queried him as to what he wanted to do for the rest of his life. Always a good question, always worthy of a good answer. For Dick Termes, a devoted artist who has been exploring his signature art form for over fifty years, his answer is a trail of over four hundred Termespheres, a testament to a dogged work ethic along a lifelong pathway. When explaining his work, he inevitably begins by noting that he is "playing with" or "playing off" one of his artistic predecessors or performing a creative experiment of his own fashioning. Whether the central dynamic is geometrical, or psychological, or philosophical, or historical, or political, Termes remains a man resolute in selecting his engaging "perfect point of artistic angle" while noting that his real pursuit is to portray "the gentle world we live in."

An anecdote from his acceptance speech when he was inducted into the South Dakota Hall of Fame further demonstrates his world view. Termes related how he conducted an experiment by cutting a large globe in half and filling one hemisphere with small balls all the same size. He motorized this basin into circular motion . . . and all the balls revolved. A short time later he was surprised to discover that the gearing of the individual balls had stopped. His curiosity piqued, he stirred the contents, and again the balls began to spin. A short time later they again went immobile. After some speculation, he added a single smaller-sized ball, stirred, engaged the power, and their turning became perpetual. His conclusion, as noted in his speech, was "the need for the oddball" to set things in motion, much as the revolutionary artist stirs up society.

Dick Termes is a revolutionary artist. The great Russian Futurist Vladimir Mayakovsky championed that "you must fight for the revolution inside yourself!" Termes has fought that good fight, and his is truly a revolving revolt. He is student and heir primarily to the design-constructing of the systems theorist Buckminster Fuller and the visual-cogitating of the printmaker M.C. Escher. Termes has lived his adult life housed in geodesic domes as a partial tribute to Fuller, and his body of work has prolifically expanded the ideational and fanciful investigations found in Escher.

Escher's son George, after visiting with Termes, expressed that it was as if he had met with the ghost of his father, and that his dad would have cherished this discussion regarding the next steps of his initial experiments. He further noted, "Dick Termes is a contemporary artist who matches my father's quest in capturing the 'un-capturable' —visual dimensions that are fascinating to ponder."[1]

Both Escher and Termes share a rapt obsession with vanishing points and optical illusions. However, Termes is much less mathematical and much more experimental with color than his predecessor. Moreover, not being bound to the flat canvas, Termes's spherical explorations have allowed for an expansive extension of the spatial contemplation found in Escher's work. Bruno Ernst, the leading expert on M.C. Escher, enthusiastically recognized: "When I was sent information about [Termes's] work, I was already stupefied. [I] never realized that painting on an actual sphere could give an entirely new visual experience hitherto unknown to me."[2]

Termes's vanishing points do not actually vanish. Roving over the spherical dimension, they double back to generate a duality of continuum. As for his optical illusions, they stun and reverberate. His traveling circumferences result in lines that each stretch out

1. George Escher, Letter to Dick Termes, n.d., in possession of Termes.

2. Bruno Ernst, email to Dick Termes, n.d.

into a halving of every sphere he draws upon. This is the terrain of Albert Einstein's curved space; Einstein said if you could see far enough you would be able to encounter the back of your own head. With Termespheres the viewer is compelled outward and inward along these multiple vectoring perspective avenues. Ironically, the most intriguing experience is that one doesn't merely look at a Termesphere; instead, the beholder looks out from them, seeing the world via a vibrant and intimate shared immediacy.

Termes's nutshell summary of his artistic approach reveals that perspective: "A Termesphere painting is an optical illusion: an inside-out view of the total physical world around you on the outside surface of a hanging and rotating sphere. Termespheres capture the up, down, and all-around visual world from one revolving point in space. Most of the time these spheres are painted on the outside so it takes a six-point perspective system to keep all of this environment around you organized."

Complex, yet organized, space. Yes. Yet far beyond that nutshell is the raw wonder of each Termesphere extending an immersive and interactive invitation. One doesn't merely view a Termesphere; one is captivated into its spinning sinuosity.

LIVING IN A ROUND WORLD

Joe Termes and Wenona Christensen-Termes resided in San Diego when Richard Alan Termes entered the world on 7 November 1941. Joe worked the shipyards, helping to create the Navy vessels soon to set sail for the Pacific Theater of World War II. With the end of the war, the Termes family returned to their hometown of Spearfish, South Dakota. Positioned within a basin just below Lookout Mountain of the majestic Black Hills, at that time this growing town held less than 3,000 people. The Termes and Christensen clans had long ago sunk their familial roots in this pristine location.

In the first decade of the twentieth century the family forebears had originally homesteaded out of tar paper shacks. The Termes side of the family broke soil near Bear Butte along the Belle Fourche River. Eventually, grandfather John Termes worked in nearby Lead as a miner in the legendary Homestake Gold Mine. The matriarch of the Christensen family, Rose, became the driving force behind the family ranch after her husband, Nels, was disabled by mustard gas in World War I. The Christensen ranch was nestled in an area known as "the lower valley." Termes fondly recalls growing up in this area of verdant gardens, roving the fields and nearby hills with his siblings and extended family of cousins, and the sound of his father framing up another Eisenhower-era boom home. Familial hijinks included piling into and on top of a shambling pickup truck with passengers calling out directions to the unlicensed and blindfolded driver as the truck crossed an open pasture, a rowdy pastime frequently put to an end by Grandma Christensen, her pioneer spirit having its carefree limits.

Spherefish (1996), A historical rendition of local history that honors
town fathers, historical buildings, and nearby landscapes.

Joe Termes, a natural builder, pursued a lifetime career in home construction. He built over thirty of his homes from the ground up, often with only his own hands. Many of these middle-class homes are still standing, and local realtors continue to remark on the high quality of the craftsmanship. Along one block, holding his houses on both sides of the street, Joe planted spruce saplings that now tower over forty feet tall.

As Joe built, Wenona took to the task of being his interior decorator while raising Dick, his older brother Joe Jr., and younger sister Judith. The family would occupy each new home until it sold. The two brothers always put up a basketball hoop and both would later play on a championship high school team. As a consequence of this ongoing home rotation, by the time Dick was eighteen the family had lived at as many different addresses in Spearfish.

Demonstrating artistic talent from an early age, Termes avidly drew and painted throughout his childhood. In the family tradition, he was a keen sportsman and hunter, but his real passion remained fixed on art. He stayed in Spearfish after high school and completed undergraduate degrees in art and education at Black Hills State University in 1964. He next answered the call to teach by accepting a post at a high school in Klamath Falls, Oregon, followed by a stint teaching art in Sheridan, Wyoming. After four years in classrooms with students K–12, Termes decided to continue his own education at the University of Wyoming, where he received his master's degree in art and first struck upon his concept of six-point perspective.

Recognizing his potential and inventive approach, in 1969 the acclaimed Otis Art Institute in Los Angeles offered him a full-ride scholarship to pursue a Master of Fine Arts. It was at Otis, steeped in innovation and fellow artists, that Termes began his conceptualization and work on spheres. Having no predecessors for his unique approach proved a challenge for the Otis instructors and classmates tasked to assess and assist him. Though isolating, his one-man path allowed for a freeing adventure into every new spherical expedition he launched. To this day his particular medium and method leaves him confessing, "I know my interests are not the interests of most artists." Regardless, he has persisted. As his MFA neared completion, Termes was already receiving invitations to show his work in galleries and museums across southern California. Despite these growing opportunities to forge a career as an artist on the West Coast, Termes opted to move back to South Dakota. The northern Black Hills remained his irresistible home.

In a return to his avocation as an educator, Termes supplemented his art sales by becoming one of the original artists to provide workshops as part of the South Dakota Arts Council's (SDAC) Artists in Schools and Communities (AISC) program. In 1972, he met a fellow SDAC artist, the accomplished puppeteer Markie Scholz of the highly regarded Dragons Are Too Seldom Puppet Theatre. The two were soon dating and in 1979 married in the Black Hills. The true son of his homebuilder father, their marital threshold led into their first Bucky Fuller geodesic dome, which Termes had handcrafted. The couple have called 1920 Christensen Drive home ever since. Again following his father's example, tall coniferous trees he planted now grace the once bare hillside. Their two sons, Lang and Kabe, joined the family in 1979 and 1985, and a first granddaughter in 2021. His cherished family stability can be summed up in Termes's assessment of his wife: "I sure was lucky to find that lady."

In 1992, the Termesphere Gallery opened as an outlier to the growing family compound of geodesic domes. Thousands of admirers and art enthusiasts the world over have since visited this space. The *New York Times* called the display area "One of the nation's most unusual art spaces!"[1] *Oprah Magazine* recognized and recommended it as "The Must-Visit" location in the state.[2]

As his catalogue continued to grow over the course of the past

1. Michael Conner, "A Red State's Arts Blues," *New York Times*, 25 April 2017.

2. "50 Ways to Love Your Summer," *Oprah Magazine*, June 2019.

five decades, Termespheres have been featured in exhibits, magazines, and book covers. His work has been displayed in over thirty-five one-man shows and fifty group shows—including those held at the Smithsonian National Air and Space Museum in Washington, D.C.; the M.C. Escher Conference in Rome; and the Sphere Museum in Tokyo. Additionally, Termes has lectured throughout the United States and internationally in England, the Netherlands, France, Germany, Italy, and at the École des Beaux-Arts in France.

The diverse appeal of his work has led to coverage and featured articles published in *Science Magazine*; *Psychological Perspectives* (published by the Carl Jung Institute); the *New York Times*; *Art Gallery International*; *The Mathematiques and Arts*; and in books that include Al Seckel's *Masters of Deception: Escher, Dali, and the Artists of Optical Illusion* and the French edition cover of Stephen Hawking's *A Brief History of Time*. His work was even featured on the cover of *Annals of Vascular Surgery* and was referenced in its featured article on the unique dimensional viewing required for angiograms.

Termes's binding dual vocation remains as an artist-educator. He says, "The approach I use to create art is similar to how I teach art. I always learn something from each piece I do. This approach also helps with the way I teach. I want the student to learn something—intellectually, emotionally, artistically—when they do one of my assignments."

Long a public art advocate, he has conducted countless workshops across the United States and Europe for all age groups. These efforts include two series of visual arts tutorial videos for South Dakota Public Broadcasting. Additionally, his collaborative work includes a series of communal mural projects completed at eighteen locations across the state.

A spectacular communal piece is located at the Little Wound School on the Pine Ridge Indian Reservation in Kyle, South Dakota. After consulting with tribal elders for their blessing and historical input, this six foot by eight foot polyhedra (a double hexagon pyramid) entitled *Lakota Headmen* was created with tribal members. Realistic portraits include Lakota women, children, and eleven historical leaders painted on a huge polyhedra tipi configuration.

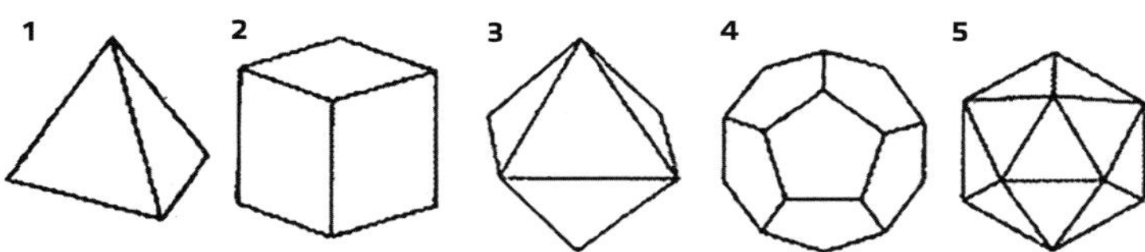

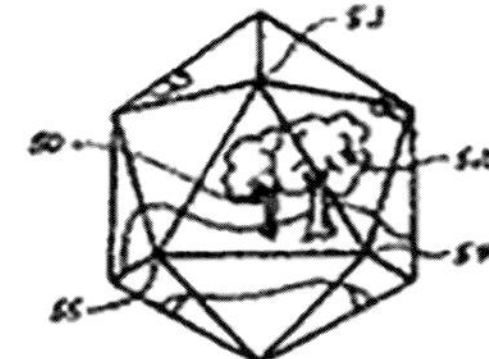

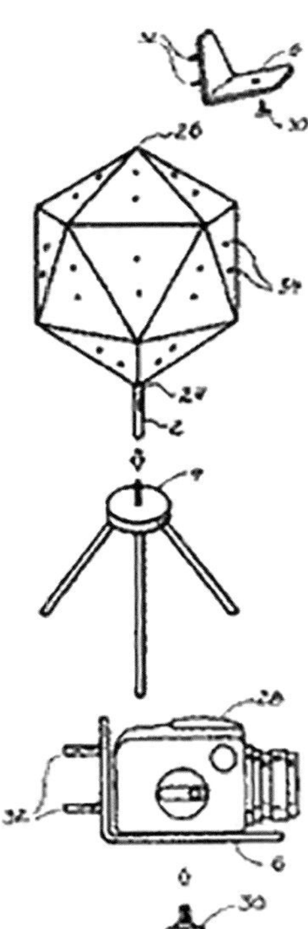

On a utilitarian quest to create a means to capture the full optics of an actual space, Termes turned inventor with his patented "Total Photo" device.

This platform mount for a camera generates an enhanced full space photographic replica, the actual surface displaying the five Platonic Solids. As he notes, "It does with photography what my spherical Termespheres do with paint. It captures the up, down and all around environment from one point in space. In the beginning I explored all five of the regular polyhedron, the tetrahedron (1), hexahedron (2), octahedron (3), dodecahedron (4), icosahedron (5)."

Termes at work in his studio.

TERMESOLOGY

Beyond sheer visual artistry, the experience of viewing a Termesphere is enriched by two governing concepts. These two interlacing latchkeys are entitled "The Concavex Phenomenon" and "The Six-Point Perspective." Together they unlock the full wonder of the optical illusion and geometric mastery that is at the core of every Termesphere.

The Concavex Phenomenon

This concept entails a visual shift in direction and shape while observing a Termesphere in rotation. The shift is generated in the pivoting consciousness of the viewer. This pivot arises in the focused witnessing of a Termesphere in motion, whereby the spherical surface appears to transform from a convex form spinning clockwise into a seemingly concave form spinning counterclockwise. The solid mass now appears to hollow out and reverse its movement. In short, it flips.

This inversion does not happen every time, and it does not happen with every viewer. It requires a fixated attention to trigger this transformation. When triggered there is an uncanny about-face that is both startling and compelling. It has even been studied and given a name by psychologists: "The Termes Illusion."[1] Termes, significantly, offers, "I've noticed that the flip happens quicker for most people when the subject matter is very realistic. In fact, the more realism in the painting, the quicker it flips." This is noteworthy, given that this toggling rearrangement is from the real into

1. Allen Barnum and Kendell C. Thornton, "Illusion of Rotary Motion Reversal in a Sphere is Facilitated by Increased Rotational Speed," *Perceptual and Motor Skills* 73, no. 2 (1991): 627–34.

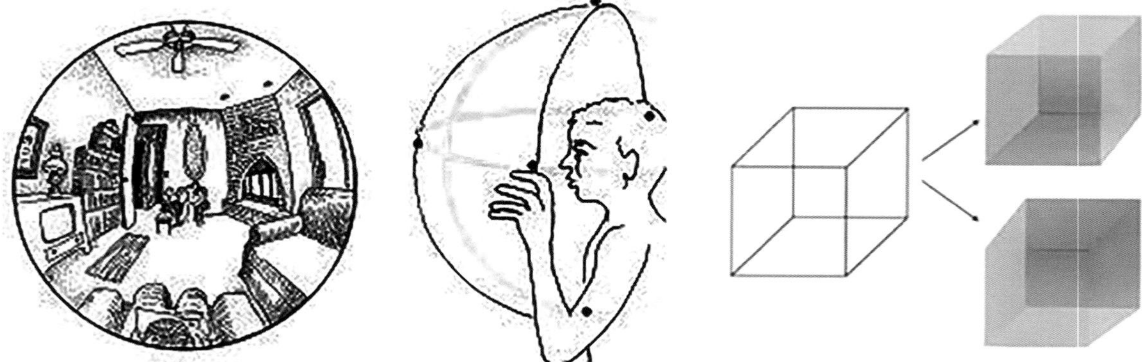

Termes says, "I also explored the pop-up polyhedron. I found with my Superwide Hasselblad camera that the dodecahedron worked the best. . . . The total photo has become a great tool for me for doing the 'famous interior' Termespheres. I believe its concept has transformed into what is now called virtual panoramic photos."

the realm of the unreal, an activated sensory conjunction for the viewer that is indeed phenomenological.

The Concavex Phenomenon is akin to the optical illusion known as the Necker Cube. Louis Necker, a Swiss crystallographer, sketched the outline of a cube without providing apparent visual cues as to its structural orientation. It can thereby appear that either the lower-left or the upper-right square is in the foreground, depending on the relative receptivity of the observer.

In the Concavex Phenomenon, both shape and movement realign within the eye and mind of the beholder. Literally and figuratively, Termes's work is all about "rounding the corners." There are no harsh, flat lines upon or within the Termesphere; each sphere possesses a world view of circular grandeur set into elegant movement. Study has verified that there is an actual auditory wave-pattern within the galaxies. The classical "music of the spheres" is now scientific fact. Watching a room of Termespheres spin—one can likewise all but hear their soundtracks.

The Six-Point Perspective

Since the Renaissance, the commonly held view of perspective has been limited along three horizontal points. The Termesphere

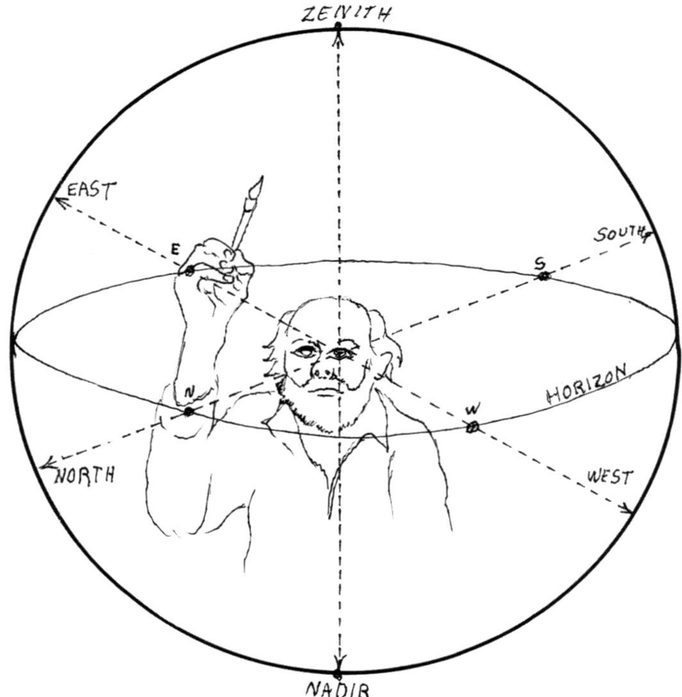

Termes describes the six point perspective as being as if he were "inside" the sphere

expands this linear triad. It merges and transcends from limited horizontals into limitless verticals.

Artists' perspectives have always been constricted to a three-point perspective by their work being rendered upon flat canvases and cramped panoramas. Termes's use of the transiting sphere allows him to centrally expand into a six-point perspective. These spinning points of observation are best denominated as north, south, east, west, zenith, and nadir. In other words, a typical painting upon a flat canvas—be it portraiture, still-life, or even abstract—is like viewing a world through a window. In a Termesphere, on the other hand, Termes's artistic goal is for each spectator to enter a new world and experience a communion via their own "personal focal point." Those personal vanishing points originate in our eyes, aligning to our individual physical position and variances of interpretive perspective. Ironically, this personalized witnessing is attained while standing on this earth, this spinning globe that the legendary systems theorist and futurist Buckminster Fuller called "Spaceship Earth." Recent virtual reality renderings of sixteen Termespheres by the award-winning photographer and digital artist Bonny Fleming make this visual event ever more accessible. Once inside the world of the Oculus goggles, each Termesphere's all-around experience is made even more manifest with uncanny delight.

Termes explains his artistic point of view when drafting and painting as being as if he is inside the sphere and crafting the outward six points on the inner side of the ball. His aim is to generate within the observer the mirrored cognition of these 360-degree optics, a mirroring conceived and painted with a goal of guiding the viewer to envision an expansive totality—depictions that are whole worlds, not merely snapshot scenes.

Termes further elucidates on his perspective construct by noting:

> In a normal Renaissance perspective all parallel lines go to the same vanishing point. In spherical perspective all parallel lines go to two points north and south or opposite poles. Think about a railroad track. The two rails which are parallel to each other vanish off in front of you to a single point. If you turn around they also project off to a single point behind you. If you add a road crossing the tracks you get two more vanishing points and if you add a telephone pole, you get the point above you and the suggestion of the point below you. Six points. This system of perspective is established by all six points being equal distant on the sphere. Every line drawn on it is actually a greater circle or in other words—divides the sphere in half.

This schemata has philosophical, even metaphysical, anteced-ents. A notable corollary is found in the teachings of Termes's South Dakota precursor, the Oglala Lakota Black Elk. As a wičáša wakáŋ (or holy man), Black Elk was a combination of psychologist, phi-losopher, and mystic. At the sight of a tumbleweed he proclaimed, "See. All things in nature long to be round." He further observed, "The power of the world always works in circles." Consider Russian icon paintings, Tibetan sand mandalas, or Jungian archetypal im-ages. Each of these visual revelations aims to illuminate, to gener-ate the healing constructs of spiritual centerings. Black Elk's grand spiritual vision reveled in the journey to focus—not to frame, not to box, but to focus. Iris down, encircle. We perceive via our eye-balls, our ocular orbs, our sighted spheres. To truly "see," as Black Elk would urge us, we are called upon to develop our own inner enlightenment. A final Black Elk revelation declared that Harney Peak (now appropriately renamed Black Elk Peak) is the center of the world, though he hastened to add that anywhere you are is the center of world. In other words, you carry your six points of outer perspective within you; you are constantly and consistently the epicenter of your unfolding world view and your own inner vision.

One might also find a final equivalence to Termespheres in the observation known as "celestial vaulting." The celestial vault is the altering bowls of the sky, whereby both the star-filled night and the blue expanse of day provide starkly different visuals. This curved arch dimension is explored in numerous cosmologies and myths from various cultures. At the scientific level, in our most recent epoch it has become frighteningly clear that every sector of our terrestrial globe affects all other sectors. Irrefutably, what goes around comes around. Flat-earthers and global warming deniers can presume otherwise, yet at a certain point even the ancients feared that "there be dragons" at our far reaches. As early as 1981, Fuller warned of the "unprecedented global catastrophe" around greenhouse gases and other environmental threats worldwide. Termes observes, "I like to talk to people about the natural properties of the sphere and its relationship to us living on the Earth. We have ignored the reality that what happens on one side of the world affects what happens on the other side. I deal with that in a visual challenge in every painting I create." The Concavex Phenomenon and the Six-Point Perspective when brought into awareness are an interwoven pair of conceptual constructs that enrich the shared experience with each and every Termesphere. The grasping of these two keys allows for the tumblers to fully turn, for new doors of perception to open. Frisson ignites. Beyond their powers of insight and perception, when we fully engage with Termespheres in their captivating spins it is nothing less than playful . . . full of play.

PART 2   Termespheres

SPHERING SOUTH DAKOTA

New discoveries continue to push back the timeline to date the first visual artists. A recent find in a limestone cave on the Indonesian island of Sulawesi reveals a visual depiction of animals dating back at least 45,500 years—more than 15,000 years older than agriculture, which originated only some 30,000 years ago. Clearly, primordial humans engaged in artistic expression long before they planted crops. Primeval cave artists could be deemed our earliest "gatherers," their harvest being the recordings and illuminations of their culture and history.

Artists likewise depicted the world of South Dakota long before the first intrusive Europeans began pushing westward. The earliest Indigenous petroglyphs found in the Black Hills date back some 8,000 years, only a few thousand years this side of the most recent ice age. Additional drawings in the cave hills of Harding County, in the state's northwest corner, include pictures of horses, whose arrival in the upper Midwest happened sometime in the mid-nineteenth century. There is also a long legacy of local Indigenous art found on hides, housing, clothing, adornments, and weaponry.

In "Dakota Sphere," Termes celebrated and depicted the broad sweep of prairies, badlands, and hills found in his native South Dakota. Its wide horizon is pulled around us with hidden images within the landscape. The top features rhythms of pictographs of prehistoric Indigenous peoples. "The whole map of South Dakota pulled into one view" was his global intention.

A fellow artist who explored the visual sweep and keynote figures of this shared homeland was the noted Yanktonai artist Oscar Howe.

**The Oscar Howe Murals at
the World's Only Corn Palace
in Mitchell, South Dakota**

Termes and Howe both won South Dakota's prestigious Governor's Award in the Arts. Howe, like Termes, would begin with a natural design and later conform his images to a central graphed pattern and thereby transform them. Beyond his paintings, for twenty-three years Howe would also use this technique to capture the large mural designs he rendered for the walls of the Corn Palace in Mitchell, South Dakota. Using colored corns, Howe's striking compositions changed annually, bringing alive illuminating visuals of celebrity portraits and landscape visages. Historically, the tradition of growing corn was a tribal staple along the Missouri River long before Euro-American farmers took up residence. Corn was and is the longstanding local king, and it was Howe who used his artistry to magnify and adorn its palace.

Dakota Sphere (South Dakota Art Museum,
Brookings, South Dakota, 1981), side view.

Dakota Sphere top view.

Termes, in similar fashion, begins with "a geometrical system to get me started. Then I let the sphere speak to me regarding potential figurative elements to be added or not."

His Dakota-themed spheres are an extensive list. They include the following images.

Rings of Time (Termesphere Gallery, 2014), A prehistoric and contemporary view of the South Dakota Badlands. It follows a concentric circle design from zenith to nadir.

Rings of Time

Rings of Time

Rings of Time

Against the Current (South Dakota Cultural Heritage Center, Pierre, South Dakota, 2003), A visualization of the Lewis and Clark expedition that originates on the lower hemisphere with St. Louis and spirals up to the Pacific Ocean on the top. Landscapes, animals, and Indigenous peoples spool out along the rotating journey.

38)

Against the Current

Deadwood: Porthole to the Past (Private Collection, 2002), A panoramic history of the old mining town including historical figures Wild Bill Hickok, Buffalo Bill Cody, and Calamity Jane.

Dakota Dome (1986), A swerving, layered vision of the
State Capitol rotunda merged to Dakota landscapes.

Matthews Opera House (2008), Painted *in situ* within the historical theatre in Spearfish, this ghostly panoramic includes scenes from plays, spectators, and famous figures who graced the stage.

Our Home (2017), An honoring of his hometown, stairs wander in and out, up and down within the mountains of Spearfish. Throughout this landscape various figures engage in a sweep of activities. The rare sphere that is not in suspended rotation, this large three-foot piece is located atop a clocktower on the Spearfish main street and is hand-cranked from below via mechanized gearing to provide its rotation.

Portrait of a College (1995), A fanciful documenting that employs a central tree festooned with faces. This commission by the library at Black Hills State College is as Termes states: "All to do with the teachers." It is also honors Termes's undergraduate alma mater and where he taught for a brief period at the beginning of his career as an educator.

Reflecting Back (Private Collection, 1989), A key exploration of six-point perspective, this is another piece painted *in situ* in the Adams House in Deadwood. This historic Victorian setting features ghost images of Mr. and Mrs. Adams manifested in quivering imagery. As Homer noted long ago, "I, for one, know of no sweeter sight for a man's eyes than his own country." An endearment that Termes clearly shares.

THE GALAXY OF SPHERINGS

Termes, the tireless experimenter, allows his central elements to overlap and evolve in the creation of his various works. Some reflect intricate interlocking tessellations, some morph and refract, some articulate outer and inner alternating images on the same spinning globe.

The physical spheres range in diameter from two inches to seven and a half feet, the typical sizes being twelve, sixteen, or twenty-four inches. Though the surface sources for his globe canvases have varied over the years, currently they are primarily repurposed light fixtures made of polyethylene and polycarbonate. After sketching in each elaborate grid, Termes uses two brushes, one to apply the acrylic paint and the second to blend the images. Thereafter, some glazing takes place, most often a scumbled opaque layer to provide an overall lightening of the hues. The completed sphere is then lacquered using an acrylic matte or gloss finish. A notable exception is the thirty-six-inch sphere mounted on the town clock on a street corner in Spearfish, South Dakota. That piece was given a clear coat treatment at a local auto body shop.

Termes takes a free-wheeling approach to the color wheel. He clearly embraces Georgia O'Keeffe's revelation that, "I found I could say things with color and shapes that I couldn't say any other way—things I had no words for."[1]

His colors frequently grade down to allow for their own vanishing values. Regarding his highly original palette, he reports:

1. Maria Popova, "Georgia O'Keeff infor tocoee on the Art of Seeing," *themarginalian*, https://www.themarginalian.org/2018/11/15/georgia-okeeffe-flower

I've long taught color theory and I experiment with all kinds of approaches to color in my paintings. Sometimes I start with finding the value differences and adding color to that later. Sometimes my sphere will launch with a single, dominant color and I play off that color with the other hues. One of my color beliefs is that there isn't such a thing as an ugly color. How this is proven is to mix what you think is a terrible color in a jar and when doing a painting use a little of this color in every color applied to the surface. It can work!

A few of my spherical paintings begin by doing a pen and ink shaded piece first and then coming back into it with tints of colors. I also like to use aerial perspective to get depth in a painting, this is frequently accentuated by my use of color. I love Georges Seurat's pointillism technique. Making the mind do the mixing with separated colors activates a painting that shimmers when you look at it. I also love the way the Impressionists consider and subtly blend color and often attempt to utilize their technique in my work.

Not a believer in those who boast of being self-taught, he acknowledges, "Why would you not want to take advantage of those who for 2,000 years have played with this?" A few of his additional forerunners include Paul Klee and Pablo Picasso. Likewise, he holds a broad appreciation of the different schools of art and allows for realist portraiture, surreal creatures and worlds, and aspects of the Gothic, Art Deco, and Abstract Expressionism to be found in his vast body of work.

Fundamentally each sphere is individually governed by an expansive core thesis that travels beyond its mathematical guiding premise into a freed work of art. Ever the skilled and patient craftsman, depending on its size and complexity, each piece can take two to three months, and even up to nine months, to fully gestate and take final form.

Beyond the home state historical spheres, categorical groupings include:

Calculating Universes

"I like to work with different geometric grid systems to see how they intermingle when applied to the sphere. Adding color to these patterns can be done in an endless number of ways. That is why these visual experiments are exciting to me."

Concentric Circles **(Termesphere Gallery, 1987).**

Global Peace (Termesphere Gallery, 2016).

Blue Spiral (Private Collection, 2003).

Subconscious Substratums

"Sometimes I like to explore the other side of my brain. Most of my work is very left-brained but this approach requires my intuition to find the answers. Loose-painting like an Abstract Expressionist work starts this process. After it dries I study the patterns and colors and

Dripping Dreams **(Termesphere Gallery, 2015).**

search for images. I bring out what I identify in hopes that others might see what I see. The whole images are not articulated, only a glimpse of what I imagine. This allows for many more of the hidden images to surface as part of the composition. I don't try to control what comes out of this, I let what appears to appear."

Bird People (Private Collection, 2014).

Fantastical Six-Point Worlds

"Strange and wonderful worlds can be held together with the six-point perspective system. This tight system of perspective can be used along with a fantasy motif to create girded and gripping

Six Senses (Private Collection, 1993).

worlds. Likewise, in my world depending on your dominant sense, that's where you go to as a vanishing point. Here is where art and physics can commingle."

Cubical Universe (Termesphere Gallery, 2010).

Concave Bubbles (Sphere Museum, Nagoya City, Japan, 2016).

The Optics of Illusion

"To look at one thing and see another is how I think of optical illusions. I find it adds another level to a painting. It also makes it so you don't memorize what you are looking at as it is always changing. One spin you see one thing and the next time another. I think this keeps the painting alive."

Eye Am A Mouth (Termesphere Gallery, 1997).

Alpha-Omega (Private Collection, 2001).

Famous Places

"There are so many wonderful architectural interior environments around the world that I feel can be best shown when wrapped upon the sphere. The problem of good design has been solved by the architects so I capture what I am seeing. How could this not be great? I traveled to France, Turkey, Italy, England, even Chicago's Wrigley Field, to find these great architectural examples and frequently utilized the total-photo platform to capture the space for later contemplation and application."

Notre Dame **(Private Collection, 1995).**

St. Peter's Basilica (Private Collection, 1997).

The Geometry of Realism

"Think of these as looking at clouds and imaging what you see. Or, rather than a cloud, you can look at different geometric patterns and do the same re-renderings. Spirals from the top of the sphere to the bottom can be turned into an endless horizon. Tight-fitting circles covering the whole sphere can be turned into images of people, trees, and snakes. Interconnecting hands can turn into people and vases. I have used this system of creating for many of my Termespheres. I think of this geometry as substructure within the painting that helps to hold the images together."

Endless Horizon (Rushmore Plaza Civic Center, Rapid City, South Dakota, 1990).

Fields and Folds of Transparency

"I love to explore what the transparent sphere will let you accomplish. When you have the inside <u>and</u> the outside surfaces of the sphere to paint — what can you do, what can you say that hasn't been said, what can you see that is at first unseen? These pieces have special designs to allow enough transparency to view the interior canvas or conversely to paint inside the images that are only

Behind the Forest (Termesphere Gallery, 2006).

62)

seen via up-close investigation. These dual dimensions can also reveal entirely different fronts and backs for the images, leaving the inside depiction totally different than that on the outside. Even the orbiting spherical shape can reveal different configurations from the inside to the structures on the outside. And the holes themselves can be spheres, access peepholes to the entirely different painting inside."

Holes to the Hole **(Private Collection, 2008)**

EPILOGUE

All the plastic arts are "Op art" —they are optical, meant to be seen and, in turn, to generate meaning, to foster understanding, to bring the tranquility of the steady state. To be really seen is to be beheld. Art can, and should be, observed via the "Third Eye," that speculative and yearning mode of transforming the visual grid into the visionary paradigm.

Beyond previously mentioned influences, Termes is likewise well aware of his predecessors in the parlance of applying arresting ambiguity via composite images of inception and deception. As early as the sixteenth century, Hans Holbein's veiled images and Giuseppe Arcimboldo's portraits modeled out of fruit and vegetables trailblazed this new artistry, this revisualizing of what can lurk along the edges of the organized mass. Then in the twentieth century Salvador Dalí and René Magritte forged scintillating and shape-shifting imagery that seared forever into the collective consciousness. Termes is indeed their grateful heir.

Moreover, he frequently gathers his subtle reveals by depicting the history and lay of the land that is South Dakota. He exalts in what he notes as the "geometry of South Dakota." The Sunshine State's visual signatures—Mount Rushmore, the Crazy Horse Memorial, the Corn Palace murals—are all the handiwork of artists. A lifelong resident, the collective of over four hundred revolving Termespheres portends to one day acquire a similar iconic stature.

Beyond his regional explorations, Termes has broadly depicted the fundamental atomic structure of all our lives. As William Blake would have it, he has seen the universes in the grains of sand. His template is innately spherical, as are we—motes of stardust nurtured in wombs.

The humble Termes never claims to conspire to such lofty aspirations. He merely states, "I don't want people to be able to walk by my work." He need not worry. It is not uncommon for someone who steps into his studio or gallery to literally stagger back. But when they enter, child or adult, they always pause, settle, behold. It is akin to hypnotism.

Near the end of his life, M.C. Escher wished for a 200-year lifespan to continue his investigative ventures. When asked if he harbors such a wish, Dick Termes shrugs and glibly responds, "I do know I want and need more time. There are still ideas in the universe to discover . . . and my art grows from that." Asked if he is contemplating retirement anytime soon, he smiles and offers, "Why would I retire from my playground?"

ACKNOWLEDGMENTS

Dick Termes and Craig Volk met as young artists/
educators in the South Dakota Arts Council's original
Sharing Company. They've been pards for over 50 years.
Not a single cross word or thrown punch from either
of them. Craig has always felt Dick's brilliance merits a
global reckoning: he is certain one day Termes's work and
gallery will be a calling to visit SoDak akin to Rushmore
and Crazy Horse (only rounder).

Heartfelt thanks from Dick and Craig to:

Dedra and Slater and the South Dakota Historical Society
Press for their work and support.

Markie, Stephanie, Claire, Ken, Kabe, Emily, Hazel,
Lang, Dylan, Jon & Noni, Roma, Alexandra, M.C.
Escher, George Escher, Bruno Ernst, all the artists in the
original SDAC Sharing Company, Carol Johnson, John
Day, Margaret Quintal, Jocelyn Hanson, Dennis Holub,
Rose Marie Tornow, Charlotte Carver, Mary Sue Siegel,
Victor Flack, David, Becky, Andy, and all the owners of
Termespheres now and in the future.